D1451541

WINTER ON THE FARM

Peggy Heeks
and Ralph Whitlock

Illustrated by Anne Howard

First published in 1985 by
Wayland (Publishers) Ltd
49 Lansdowne Place, Hove
East Sussex BN3 1HF, England

© Copyright 1985 Wayland (Publishers) Ltd

ISBN 0 85078 532 4

Filmset by
Latimer Trend & Company Ltd, Plymouth
Printed in Italy by
G. Canale & C.S.p.A., Turin
Bound in the UK by The Pitman Press, Bath

Contents

Winter is the coldest time of the year.
There is not much sunshine
and the days get dark early.
Most of the trees have no leaves
and the fields are bare.
Winter is a harsh time to be working outdoors.

5

In winter the farmer is kept busy
looking after the farm animals.
When the weather gets very cold
he moves some of the animals into barns.
The calves have small pens
with straw for bedding.
The bull has a large pen with a way out
to the water trough in the yard.
The horses are taken out for exercise each day.
They stay in the warm stables the rest of the time.

Sheep spend most of the year outdoors.
Their thick fleeces keep them warm in winter.
But snow can be dangerous for sheep.
It covers the grass so the sheep cannot find food.
Sheep often get lost in deep snow drifts.
Then the farmer has to search for the lost sheep.
Sometimes sheep get buried in the snow and die.
This farmer has brought some hay to his sheep
so that they will have dry food to eat.

9

In winter the farm animals need
extra food to keep warm.
There is not much fresh grass for them to eat
so the farmer has to give them other food.
In this picture the farmer is bringing hay,
silage and turnips for the cows to eat.

Many families eat roast turkey
for their Christmas dinner.
In the picture you can see the
farmer's flock of turkeys.
They are given plenty of food to make them fat.
Before Christmas the turkeys will be killed
and sent to the shops to be sold.

The farmer likes to finish most
of the ploughing in autumn.
Some crops ripen late so the farmer
has to wait and plough in winter.
The tractor in the picture has
started ploughing in a field where
the cows are eating the last strip of kale.
The plough buries weeds and
breaks up big lumps of soil.

Winter is the time when the farmer repairs
the farm buildings or makes new ones.
These men are building a new cattle shed.
The old shed had an earth floor.
It got very muddy.
The new shed has a concrete floor.
The farmer will be able to wash
the concrete floor with a hose and keep it clean.

17

The farmer needs to drain his land
so that the rain-water can soak away.
He digs ditches around his fields.
Old ditches get blocked with leaves,
twigs and mud.
Ditches and drains are cleaned out in winter
and new ones are dug.
This is done with large machines
called mechanical diggers.

In winter the farmer has time
to mend the farm's fences and hedges.
Hedges are made by weaving the branches
of bushes together.
Most fences are made of barbed wire and
wooden posts.
The fences and hedges keep the animals from
straying away from the farm or
into fields where crops are growing.
The men in the picture are making a new fence.

In winter the farmer makes plans for the new year.
He decides what to grow in each field.
He decides which seeds to buy.
He decides if he needs to buy more animals
and new machines.
He looks at magazines and catalogues
to help him plan what to do.

Animals need special care in winter.
The farmer often checks them to make sure
that they are healthy.
The farmer always keeps some medicines
at the farm to cure simple illnesses.
If an animal is very ill the farmer will ask
the vet to come and help the animal get better.
The cow in the picture is having
an injection from the vet.

Many farm animals are kept indoors all the year.
They live in buildings that are always
warm and brightly lit.
They do not know whether it is spring, summer,
autumn or winter outside.

These pigs are kept for their meat.
They are given lots of food
to make them grow quickly.
Then the farmer sells them at the market.

Wild animals and birds need lots of food in winter, just like farm animals do.

In cold weather there is less food for them to eat.

Sometimes these birds and animals try to eat the food that the farmer is storing for his cattle.

The farmer has to protect his crops and stores from rats, mice, rabbits, pigeons and deer.

Foxes sometimes kill the farmer's chickens.

The farmer puts poison down to kill the animals. Sometimes he has to shoot them.

Rabbit

Rat

Pigeon

Mice

Fox

Deer

29

We like to have fresh food all the year round.
There are still a few crops in the fields in winter.
There are carrots, parsnips, leeks and cabbages.
Some farmers have large greenhouses so they can
grow fruit and vegetables even when it is cold.
Tomatoes are growing in this warm greenhouse.
It is expensive to keep the greenhouse
warm through the winter.
But the farmer gets a good price for the food
he grows there.

31

Glossary

Barbed wire   Wire with sharp spikes on it,
   used for making fences.
Bulls   Male cattle.
Catalogue   A list of things.
Fleece   A sheep's woolly coat.
Greenhouse   A glass building where plants are grown.
Kale   A leafy crop grown as food for cattle and sheep.
Pen   A small area surrounded by fences so that
   animals can be kept there.
Silage   Animal food made from freshly cut grass.
Trough   A long, narrow container that holds
   water or food for farm animals.
Winter   The coldest time of the year,
   between autumn and spring.
   In the northern countries of the world
   winter is in December, January and February.
   In the southern countries of the world
   Winter is in June, July and August.
Vet   Someone whose job is to help sick and
   injured animals to get better.
Snow drift   A bank of deep snow.

Index

Acknowledgements
The publishers would like to thank *Farmers Weekly* and the National Farmers Union for supplying reference material for the illustrations in this book.